Dr. Carlson does the Church an important service by showing Christians what the Bible says about the future of Israel and teaching them how to pray for Israel. I recommend this to readers wanting to learn about and pray for Israel.

—**GERALD MCDERMOTT,**
author of *Israel Matters*, editor of *The New Christian Zionism*
and *Understanding the Jewish Roots of Christianity*

We highly recommend Christopher Carlson's book *Jerusalem Prayers*. Excellent way Dr. Carlson has gathered Scriptures to express the heart of God for His treasured people. This assures us we are praying in the will of God.

—**MERRILL AND DONNA BOLENDER,**
Indiana Representatives for Operation Exodus USA

Every line written about Israel and God's care for His land and its people is important and useful for us. *Jerusalem Prayers: 31 Daily Scriptures Selections and Prayers for Israel* will be an inspiration to many and draw us all to deeper commitment to praying for the fulfillment of all of God's plan for Israel. "Pray for the peace of Jerusalem! May they prosper who love you." (Psalm 122:6)

—**DR. LARRY EHRLICH,**
USA director of Jerusalem Cornerstone Foundation

Jerusalem Prayers

31 Daily Scripture Selections and Prayers
for Israel and the Jewish People

Christopher Carlson

For Dad
On his 98th birthday

Who passed on to us
God's heart for Israel

Thank you!

Contents

Introduction

"On your walls, O Jerusalem, I have set watchmen;
all the day and all the night they shall never be silent.
You who put the Lord in remembrance,
take no rest and give him no rest
until he establishes Jerusalem
and makes it a praise in the earth."

— Isaiah 62:6–7

This book started as a way to organize prayers for Israel, having read the Isaiah passage above and understood that to "put the Lord in remembrance" meant simply to remind him of what he had said in his Word regarding Israel. So, I searched the Scriptures and organized the verses around the themes that emerged. The Scriptures were then formulated into prayers to express to God what he had already declared and promised. And that's what you have before you in this book: Scriptures and prayers. Simple.

Finally ready, a copy of this project was given to my Dad for his 98th birthday — that was 2019. He lived another year and a half during which time he read and prayed from it most days.

And he would repeatedly exclaim, "You should by all means publish this, say!" Well, I'm finally doing just that . . .

I pray that it is a blessing to you. And through your prayers, a blessing to Israel, Jerusalem and the Jewish people.

— Christopher Carlson

All the Earth Blessed

Day 1 Scriptures

"In your [Abraham's] offspring shall all the nations of the earth be blessed, because you have obeyed my voice." — The earth shall be full of the knowledge of the LORD as the waters cover the sea. — Nations will fear the name of the LORD, and all the kings of the earth will fear your glory. For the LORD builds up Zion. — Until her righteousness goes forth as brightness, and her salvation as a burning torch . . . until he establishes Jerusalem and makes it a praise in the earth. The nations shall see your righteousness. — This gospel of the kingdom will be proclaimed throughout the whole world as a testimony to all nations, and then the end will come. — Until the fullness of the Gentiles has come in. — That your way may be known on earth, your saving power among all nations. Let the peoples praise you, O God; let all the peoples praise you! Let the nations be glad and sing for joy. — Behold, a great multitude that no one could number, from every nation, from all tribes and peoples and languages, standing before the throne and before the Lamb. — Now the LORD said to Abram . . . "in you all the families of the earth shall be blessed."

GEN. 22:18. ISA. 11:9. PSA. 102:16. ISA 62:1,7,2. MATT 24:14. ROM 11:25. PSA. 67:2–4. REV. 7:9. GEN. 12:1,3.

All the Earth Blessed

Day 1 Prayer[*]

Thank you, Father, that in Abraham all the nations of the earth shall be blessed; that the earth shall be full of the knowledge of the Lord as the waters cover the sea; that nations will fear the name of the Lord, and all the kings of the earth will fear your glory, for you build up Zion. Thank you that Zion's righteousness shall go forth as brightness and her salvation as a burning torch. Thank you that the gospel of the kingdom shall be proclaimed throughout the whole world as a testimony to all the nations, that the fullness of the Gentiles shall come in. So, we pray that your way may be known on earth, your saving power among all nations. Thank you for the great multitude John saw that no one could number, from every nation, from all tribes and peoples and languages, standing before your throne and before the Lamb. So let the peoples praise you, O God; let all the peoples praise you! Let the nations be glad and sing for joy! For in Abraham shall all the families of the earth be blessed. Thank you, Father.

---

[*] Each day has corresponding "Listening Prayer Impressions" in the Appendix

Apple of His Eye

Day 2 Scriptures

The LORD's portion is his people, Jacob his allotted heritage. "He found him in a desert land, and in the howling waste of the wilderness; he encircled him, he cared for him, he kept him as the apple of his eye." — My son, keep my words and treasure up my commandments with you; keep my commandments and live; keep my teaching as the apple of your eye. — Keep me as the apple of your eye; hide me in the shadow of your wings, from the wicked who do me violence, my deadly enemies who surround me. — For thus said the LORD of hosts, after his glory sent me to the nations who plundered you, for he who touches you touches the apple of his eye: "Behold, I will shake my hand over them, and they shall become plunder for those who served them. Then you will know that the LORD of hosts has sent me."

Deut. 32:9–10. Prov. 7:1–2. Psa. 17:8–9. Zech. 2:8–9.

Apple of His Eye

Day 2 Prayer

Father, your portion is your people, Jacob your allotted heritage, whom you found in a desert land, and in the howling waste of the wilderness. You encircled him, cared for him and kept him as the apple of your eye. So, may Israel, your son, keep your words and treasure up your commandments; keep your commandments and live; keep your teaching as the apple of his eye. And, Father, may you keep him as the apple of your eye. So hide him in the shadow of your wings from the wicked who do him violence, his deadly enemies who surround him. For he who touches him touches the apple of your eye. Yes, your portion is your people, Jacob your allotted heritage. Bless you, Father.

Appointed Time to Favor
Day 3 Scriptures

But you, O Lord, are enthroned forever; you are remembered throughout all generations. You will arise and have pity on Zion; it is the time to favor her; the appointed time has come. — Therefore the Lord waits to be gracious to you, and therefore he exalts himself to show mercy to you. For the Lord is a God of justice; blessed are all those who wait for him.For a people shall dwell in Zion, in Jerusalem; you shall weep no more. He will surely be gracious to you at the sound of your cry. As soon as he hears it, he answers you. — O LORD, be gracious to us; we wait for you. Be our arm every morning, our salvation in the time of trouble. — May God be gracious to us and bless us and make his face to shine upon us, Selah, that your way may be known on earth, your saving power among all nations. — On your walls, O Jerusalem, I have set watchmen; all the day and all the night they shall never be silent. You who put the LORD in remembrance, take no rest, and give him no rest until he establishes Jerusalem and makes it a praise in the earth.

Psa. 102:12–13. Isa. 30:18–19; 33:2. Psa. 67:1–2. Isa. 62:6–7.

Appointed Time to Favor
Day 3 Prayer

Thank you, Father, that you will arise and have pity on Zion, for the appointed time has come; it is the time to favor her. For you wait to be gracious to her, and you exalt yourself to show mercy to her; as you are a God of justice, blessed are all those who wait for you. Indeed, a people shall dwell in Zion, in Jerusalem, who shall weep no more; to whom you will surely be gracious at the sound of their cry. As soon as you hear it, you will answer. O Lord, be gracious to them; they wait for you. Be their arm every morning, their salvation in the time of trouble. May you, O God, be gracious to them and bless them and make your face to shine upon them, that your way may be known on earth, your saving power among all nations. Yes, we put you in remembrance, and give you no rest until you establish Jerusalem and make it a praise in the earth. For you, O Lord, are enthroned forever; you are remembered throughout all generations. You will arise and have pity on Zion; it is the time to favor her; the appointed time has come. Bless you, Father!

Arise

Day 4 Scriptures

You will arise and have pity on Zion; it is the time to favor her; the appointed time has come. — Arise, O God, defend your cause. — Arise, O LORD; O God, lift up your hand; forget not the afflicted. — "Because the poor are plundered, because the needy groan, I will now arise," says the LORD; "I will place him in the safety for which he longs." — Covenants are broken; cities are despised; there is no regard for man. The land mourns and languishes . . . "Now I will arise," says the LORD, "now I will lift myself up; now I will be exalted. — Awake, awake, put on strength, O arm of the LORD; awake, as in days of old, the generations of long ago. — Arise, O LORD! Let not man prevail; let the nations be judged before you! — Arise, O God, judge the earth; for you shall inherit all the nations! — Awake, awake, put on your strength, O Zion; put on your beautiful garments, O Jerusalem, the holy city. — Arise, shine, for your light has come, and the glory of the LORD has risen upon you. For behold, darkness shall cover the earth, and thick darkness the peoples; but the LORD will arise upon you, and his glory will be seen upon you.

Psa. 102:13, 74:22, 10:12, 12:5. Isa. 33:8–10, 51:9.
Psa. 9:19, 82:8. Isa. 52:1, 60:2.

Arise

Day 4 Prayer

Thank you, Father, that you will arise and have pity on Zion. You will arise, O God, and defend your cause. You will arise, O Lord, and lift up your hand; you will not forget the afflicted. Because the poor are plundered and the needy groan, you will arise and place them in the safety for which they long. When covenants are broken, cities are despised, there is no regard for man and the land mourns and languishes, you will arise, you will lift yourself up, you will be exalted. You will awaken, O arm of the Lord, and put on strength as in the days of old, the generations of long ago. You will arise, O Lord, and not let man prevail, for the nations shall be judged before you. Yes, you will arise, O God, and judge the earth, for you shall inherit all the nations.

Awake, awake, put on your strength, O Zion; put on your beautiful garments, O Jerusalem, the holy city. Arise, shine, for your light has come, and the glory of the Lord has risen upon you. For behold darkness shall cover the earth, and thick darkness the peoples; but the Lord shall arise upon you, and his glory shall be seen upon you. Alleluia!

Beloved

Day 5 Scriptures

For the Lord takes pleasure in his people; he adorns the humble with salvation. — For the LORD will not forsake his people, for his great name's sake, because it has pleased the LORD to make you a people for himself. — He found him in a desert land, and in the howling waste of the wilderness; he encircled him, he cared for him, he kept him as the apple of his eye. — He brought me out into a broad place; he rescued me, because he delighted in me. — I ask, then, has God rejected his people? By no means! — As regards the gospel, they are enemies for your sake. But as regards election, they are beloved for the sake of their forefathers. For the gifts and the calling of God are irrevocable. — The LORD hath appeared of old unto me, saying, Yea, I have loved thee with an everlasting love: therefore with lovingkindness have I drawn thee.

PSA. 149:4. 1 SAM. 12:22. DEUT. 32:10. PSA. 18:19.
ROM. 11:1, 28–29. JER. 31:3 (KJV).

Beloved

DAY 5 PRAYER

Thank you, Father, that you take pleasure in your people; you adorn the humble with salvation. It pleased you to make Israel a people for yourself. You found him in a desert land and in the howling wilderness; you encircled him, you cared for him, you kept him as the apple of your eye. You rescued him because you delighted in him. By no means have you rejected your people; even though as regards the gospel they are your enemies, yet as regards election they are beloved for the sake of their forefathers, because your gifts and your calling are irrevocable. You have loved them with an everlasting love, therefore with lovingkindness have you drawn them; for you take pleasure in your people, you adorn the humble with salvation. Bless you, Lord.

Chosen

Day 6 Scriptures

For the LORD has chosen Jacob for himself, Israel as his own possession. — You are the LORD, the God who chose Abram and brought him out of Ur of the Chaldeans and gave him the name Abraham. — But you, Israel, my servant, Jacob, whom I have chosen, the offspring of Abraham, my friend; you whom I took from the ends of the earth, and called from its farthest corners, saying to you, "You are my servant, I have chosen you and not cast you off"; fear not, for I am with you. — He loved your fathers and chose their offspring after them and brought you out of Egypt with his own presence, by his great power, driving out before you nations greater and mightier than you, to bring you in, to give you their land for an inheritance, as it is this day. — Behold, to the LORD your God belong heaven and the heaven of heavens, the earth with all that is in it. Yet the LORD set his heart in love on your fathers and chose their offspring after them, you above all peoples, as you are this day. — "For you are a people holy to the LORD your God. The LORD your God has chosen you to be a people for his treasured possession, out of all the peoples who are on the face of the earth. It was not because you were more in number than any other people that the LORD set his love on you and chose you, for you were the fewest of all peoples, but it is because the LORD loves you and is keeping the oath that he swore to your fathers. — So too at the present time there is a remnant, chosen by grace.

Psa. 135:4. Neh. 9:7. Isa. 41:8–10. Deut. 4:37–38; 10:14–15; 7:6–8. Rom. 11:5.

Chosen

DAY 6 PRAYER

Thank you, Father, that you have chosen Israel as your own possession. You chose Abram and brought him out of Ur of the Chaldeans and gave him the name Abraham. And to Israel you say: "You are my servant, I have chosen you and not cast you off; fear not for I am with you." For you loved Israel's fathers and chose their offspring after them and brought them out of Egypt. To you, O Lord, belong heaven and the heaven of heavens, the earth with all that is in it; yet you set your heart in love on Israel and chose them above all peoples. They are a people holy to you, chosen to be a people for your treasured possession. It was not because they were more in number than any other people that you set your love on them and chose them, for they were the fewest of all peoples; but it was because you loved them and were keeping the oath that you swore to their fathers. Even at the present time there is a remnant chosen by grace. For you have chosen Jacob for yourself, Israel as your own possession. Alleluia!

Cleansing

Day 7 Scriptures

"And I will pour upon the house of David, and upon the inhabitants of Jerusalem, the spirit of grace and of supplications . . . On that day there shall be a fountain opened for the house of David and the inhabitants of Jerusalem, to cleanse them from sin and uncleanness." — "I will take you from the nations and gather you from all the countries and bring you into your own land. I will sprinkle clean water on you, and you shall be clean from all your uncleannesses, and from all your idols I will cleanse you." — "I will restore the fortunes of Judah and the fortunes of Israel, and rebuild them as they were at first. I will cleanse them from all the guilt of their sin against me, and I will forgive all the guilt of their sin and rebellion against me." — "Come now, let us reason together, says the LORD: though your sins are like scarlet, they shall be as white as snow; though they are red like crimson, they shall become like wool. — If we confess our sins, he is faithful and just to forgive us our sins and to cleanse us from all unrighteousness.

Zech. 12:10 (KJV); 13:1. Ezek. 36:24–25. Jer. 33:7–8. Isa. 1:18. 1 John 1:9.

Cleansing

Day 7 Prayer

Thank you, Father, that you will pour out on the house of David and the inhabitants of Jerusalem a spirit of grace and of supplications, and there will be a fountain opened for them to cleanse them from sin and uncleanness. You will sprinkle clean water on them and they shall be clean from all their uncleannesses, and from all their idols you will cleanse them. You will cleanse them from all the guilt of their sin against you and forgive all the guilt of their sin and rebellion against you. Though their sins are like scarlet, they shall be as white as snow; though they are red like crimson, they shall become like wool. For if we confess our sins you are faithful and just to forgive us our sins and to cleanse us from all unrighteousness. Thank you, Father.

Comfort

Day 8 Scriptures

Comfort, comfort my people, says your God. Speak tenderly to Jerusalem, and cry to her that her warfare is ended, that her iniquity is pardoned. — For the LORD comforts Zion; he comforts all her waste places and makes her wilderness like Eden, her desert like the garden of the LORD; joy and gladness will be found in her, thanksgiving and the voice of song. — "'Thus says the LORD of hosts: My cities shall again overflow with prosperity, and the LORD will again comfort Zion and again choose Jerusalem.'" — He who scattered Israel will gather him, and will keep him as a shepherd keeps his flock . . . They shall come and sing aloud on the height of Zion, and they shall be radiant over the goodness of the LORD . . . I will turn their mourning into joy; I will comfort them, and give them gladness for sorrow." — "As one whom his mother comforts, so I will comfort you; you shall be comforted in Jerusalem.".

Isa. 40:1–2; 51:3. Zech. 1:17. Jer. 31:10, 12, 13. Isa. 66:13.

Comfort

Day 8 Prayer

Thank you, Father, that you comfort your people; you speak tenderly to Jerusalem that her warfare is ended, that her iniquity is pardoned. For you comfort Zion; you comfort all her waste places and make her wilderness like Eden, her desert like the garden of the Lord; joy and gladness will be found in her, thanksgiving and the voice of song. Your cities, O Lord, shall again overflow with prosperity and you will again comfort Zion and again choose Jerusalem. You who scattered Israel will gather him and will keep him as a shepherd keeps his flock; they shall come and sing aloud on the height of Zion, and they shall be radiant over your goodness, O Lord. You will turn their mourning into joy; you will comfort them and give them gladness for sorrow. As one whom his mother comforts, so you will comfort them, and they shall be comforted in Jerusalem. Bless you, Father!

Deliverance

Day 9 Scriptures

"Like birds hovering, so the LORD of hosts will protect Jerusalem; he will protect and deliver it; he will spare and rescue it." — "You will not need to fight in this battle. Stand firm, hold your position, and see the salvation of the LORD on your behalf, O Judah and Jerusalem.' Do not be afraid and do not be dismayed." — You are a hiding place for me; you preserve me from trouble; you surround me with shouts of deliverance. — Many times he delivered them . . . he looked upon their distress, when he heard their cry. For their sake he remembered his covenant, and relented according to the abundance of his steadfast love. — For he will deliver you from the snare of the fowler and from the deadly pestilence. He will cover you with his pinions, and under his wings you will find refuge; his faithfulness is a shield and buckler. — "Call upon me in the day of trouble; I will deliver you, and you shall glorify me." — For he delivers the needy when he calls, the poor and him who has no helper. — Behold, the eye of the LORD is on those who fear him, on those who hope in his steadfast love, that he may deliver their soul from death and keep them alive in famine. — "The Deliverer will come from Zion."

Isa 31:5. 2 Chron. 20:17.
Psa. 32:7, 106:43–45, 91:3–4, 50:15, 72:12, 33:18–19. Rom.11:26.

Deliverance

Day 9 Prayer

Thank you, Father, that like birds hovering, you will protect Jerusalem; you will protect and deliver it; you will spare and rescue it.

O Judah and Jerusalem, you will not need to fight in this battle; stand firm, hold your position, and see the salvation of the Lord on your behalf. Do not be afraid and do not be dismayed.

Yes, you, O Lord, are a hiding place; you preserve them from trouble; you surround them with shouts of deliverance. Many times you delivered them; you looked upon their distress when you heard their cry; for their sake you remembered your covenant and relented according to the abundance of your steadfast love. For you will deliver them from the snare of the fowler and from the deadly pestilence; you will cover them with your pinions, and under your wings they will find refuge; your faithfulness is a shield and buckler. When they call upon you in the day of trouble you will deliver them and they shall glorify you. For you deliver the needy when he calls; the poor and him who has no helper. Behold, your eye, O Lord, is on those who fear you, on those who hope in your steadfast love, that you may deliver their soul from death and keep them alive in famine. Indeed, the Deliverer will come from Zion. Bless you, Father!

Dwell

The Lord dwells in Zion. — For the Lord has chosen Zion; he has desired it for his dwelling place: "This is my resting place forever; here I will dwell, for I have desired it." — I the Lord dwell in the midst of the people of Israel. — "I will dwell among the people of Israel and will be their God. And they shall know that I am the Lord their God, who brought them out of the land of Egypt that I might dwell among them." — The Lord, the God of Israel . . . dwells in Jerusalem forever. — In Judah God is known; his name is great in Israel. His abode has been established in Salem, his dwelling place in Zion. — You shall know that I am the Lord your God, who dwells in Zion, my holy mountain." — "I have returned to Zion and will dwell in the midst of Jerusalem . . . Old men and old women shall again sit in the streets of Jerusalem, each with staff in hand because of great age. And the streets of the city shall be full of boys and girls playing in its streets." — "My dwelling place shall be with them, and I will be their God, and they shall be my people. Then the nations will know that I am the Lord who sanctifies Israel, when my sanctuary is in their midst forevermore."

Joel 3:21. Psa. 132:13–14. Num. 35:34. Ex. 29:45–46. I Chron. 23:25. Psa. 76:1–2. Joel 3:17. Zech.8:3–5. Ezek. 37:27–28.

Dwell

Day 10 Prayer

Thank you, Father, that you dwell in Zion. For you have chosen Zion, you have desired it for your dwelling place, your resting place forever. You the Lord dwell in the midst of the people of Israel; you brought them out of the land of Egypt that you might dwell among them. You dwell in Jerusalem forever; your abode has been established in Salem, your dwelling place in Zion. Indeed, they shall know that you are the Lord their God who dwells in Zion, your holy mountain. Yes, you have returned to Zion and will dwell in the midst of Jerusalem, and old men and old women shall again sit in the streets of Jerusalem, and the streets of the city shall be full of boys and girls playing in its streets. Your dwelling place shall be with them, and you will be their God, and they shall be your people. Then the nations shall know that you are the Lord who sanctifies Israel, when your sanctuary is in their midst forevermore. Alleluia!

Forgiveness

Day 11 Scriptures

"I will restore Israel to his pasture . . . In those days and in that time, declares the Lord, iniquity shall be sought in Israel, and there shall be none. And sin in Judah, and none shall be found, for I will pardon those whom I leave as a remnant." — "If my people who are called by my name humble themselves, and pray and seek my face and turn from their wicked ways, then I will hear from heaven and will forgive their sin and heal their land." — If you, O Lord, should mark iniquities, O Lord, who could stand? But with you there is forgiveness, that you may be feared . . . O Israel, hope in the Lord! For with the Lord there is steadfast love, and with him is plentiful redemption. And he will redeem Israel from all his iniquities. — They refused to obey and were not mindful of the wonders . . . But you are a God ready to forgive, gracious and merciful, slow to anger and abounding in steadfast love, and did not forsake them. — To the Lord our God belong mercy and forgiveness. — "Behold, the days are coming, declares the Lord, when I will make a new covenant with the house of Israel and the house of Judah . . . I will put my law within them, and I will write it on their hearts . . . I will forgive their iniquity, and I will remember their sin no more." — "I will cleanse them from all the guilt of their sin against me, and I will forgive all the guilt of their sin and rebellion against me." — A partial hardening has come upon Israel, until the fullness of the Gentiles has come in. And in this way all Israel will be saved, as it is written: "The Deliverer will come from Zion, He will banish ungodliness from Jacob"; "and this will be my covenant with them when I take away their sins."

JER. 50:19,20. 2 CHRON. 7:14. PSA. 130:3–4, 7–8. NEH. 9:17. DAN. 9:9.
JER. 31: 31, 33, 34. JER. 33:8. ROM. 11:25–27.

Forgiveness

Day 11 Prayer

Father, thank you that when you restore Israel to his pasture, iniquity shall be sought in him and there shall be none; and sin in Judah, and none shall be found, for you will pardon those whom you leave as a remnant. Thank you that if your people who are called by your name humble themselves and pray and seek your face and turn from their wicked ways, then you will hear from heaven and will forgive their sin and heal their land. For if you, O Lord, should mark iniquities, O Lord, who could stand? But with you there is forgiveness, that you may be feared. So, Israel is to hope in you! For with you there is steadfast love and with you is plentiful redemption, and you will redeem Israel from all his iniquities. Even when they refuse to obey and are not mindful of your wonders, you are a God ready to forgive and merciful, slow to anger and abounding in steadfast love, and will not forsake them. For to you belong mercy and forgiveness. Thank you for the new covenant with the house of Israel and the house of Judah in which you put your law within them and write it on their hearts; you forgive their iniquity and remember their sin no more. You cleanse them from all the guilt of their sin and rebellion against you. Yes, you, the Deliverer, will come from Zion, you will banish ungodliness from Jacob; and this will be your covenant with them when you take away their sins. Thank you, Father.

God Faithful to His Word
Day 12 Scriptures

Forever, O LORD, your word is firmly fixed in the heavens. — The grass withers, the flower fades, but the word of our God will stand forever. — Heaven and earth will pass away, but my words will not pass away. — Not one word of all the good promises that the LORD had made to the house of Israel had failed; all came to pass. — Thus says the LORD, who gives the sun for light by day and the fixed order of the moon and the stars for light by night . . .:"If this fixed order departs from before me, declares the LORD, then shall the offspring of Israel cease from being a nation before me forever." — "Thus says the LORD of hosts: Behold, I will save my people from the east country and from the west country, and I will bring them to dwell in the midst of Jerusalem. And they shall be my people, and I will be their God, in faithfulness and in righteousness." — Your steadfast love, O LORD, extends to the heavens, your faithfulness to the clouds. — But you, O Lord, are a God merciful and gracious, slow to anger and abounding in steadfast love and faithfulness. — He has remembered his steadfast love and faithfulness to the house of Israel.

Psa. 119:89. Isa. 40:8. Luke 21:33. Josh. 21:45. Jer. 31:35–36.
Zech. 8:7–8. Psa. 36:5, 86:15, 98:3.

God Faithful to His Word

Day 12 Prayer

Thank you, Father, that your word is firmly fixed in the heavens, that the grass withers and the flower fades, but your word will stand forever. Thank you that though heaven and earth pass away, your words will not pass away. Thank you that not one word of all the good promises you made to the house of Israel failed, all came to pass. For you said, you, who give the sun for light by day and the fixed order of the moon and the stars for light by night, "If this fixed order departs from before me, then shall the offspring of Israel cease from being a nation before me forever." You said you will save your people from the east country and from the west country, and you will bring them to dwell in the midst of Jerusalem; and they shall be your people and you will be their God, in faithfulness and righteousness. Your steadfast love, O Lord, extends to the heavens, your faithfulness to the clouds. You are a God merciful and gracious, slow to anger and abounding in steadfast love and faithfulness. Yes, you have remembered your steadfast love and faithfulness to the house of Israel. Bless you, Father!

Goodness

Day 13 Scriptures

I will recount the steadfast love of the LORD, the praises of the LORD, according to all that the LORD has granted us, and the great goodness to the house of Israel that he has granted them according to his compassion, according to the abundance of his steadfast love. — Then Moses told his father-in-law all that the LORD had done to Pharaoh and to the Egyptians for Israel's sake, all the hardship that had come upon them in the way, and how the LORD had delivered them. And Jethro rejoiced for all the good that the LORD had done to Israel, in that he had delivered them out of the hand of the Egyptians. — And they captured fortified cities and a rich land, and took possession of houses full of all good things, cisterns already hewn, vineyards, olive orchards and fruit trees in abundance. So they ate and were filled and became fat and delighted themselves in your great goodness. — One generation shall commend your works to another, and shall declare your mighty acts. On the glorious splendor of your majesty, and on your wondrous works, I will meditate. They shall speak of the might of your awesome deeds, and I will declare your greatness. They shall pour forth the fame of your abundant goodness and shall sing aloud of your righteousness. — I will make with them an everlasting covenant, that I will not turn away from doing good to them. And I will put the fear of me in their hearts, that they may not turn from me. I will rejoice in doing them good, and I will plant them in this land in faithfulness, with all my heart and all my soul. — And this city shall be to me a name of joy, a praise and a glory before all the nations of the earth who shall hear of all the good that I do for them. They shall fear and tremble because of all the good and all the prosperity I provide for it. — Truly God is good to Israel, to those who are pure in heart.

Isa 63:7. Ex. 18:8–9. Neh. 9:25. Ps. 145:4–7. Jer. 32:40–41. Jer. 33:9. Ps. 73:1.

Goodness

Day 13 Prayer

Thank you, Father, for your great goodness to the house of Israel that you have granted them according to your compassion, according to the abundance of your steadfast love. For you delivered them out of the hand of the Egyptians and they captured fortified cities and a rich land and took possession of houses full of all good things, cisterns already hewn, vineyards, olive orchards and fruit trees in abundance, and delighted themselves in your great goodness. One generation shall commend your works to another and shall declare your mighty acts; they shall pour forth the fame of your abundant goodness and shall sing aloud of your righteousness. And you will make with them an everlasting covenant that you will not turn away from doing good to them. You will put the fear of you in their hearts that they may not turn from you. You will rejoice in doing them good, and you will plant them in the land in faithfulness, with all your heart and with all your soul. And Jerusalem shall be to you a name of joy, a praise and a glory before all the nations of the earth who shall hear of all the good that you do for them. They shall fear and tremble because of all the good and all the prosperity you provide for it. Truly you are good to Israel, to those who are pure in heart. Thank you, Father.

Humility

Day 14 Scriptures

For you save a humble people, but the haughty eyes you bring down. — And you shall remember the whole way that the LORD your God has led you these forty years in the wilderness, that he might humble you, testing you to know what was in your heart, whether you would keep his commandments or not . . . who fed you in the wilderness with manna that your fathers did not know, that he might humble you and test you, to do you good in the end. — "He has shown strength with his arm; he has scattered the proud in the thoughts of their hearts; he has brought down the mighty from their thrones and exalted those of humble estate; he has filled the hungry with good things, and the rich he has sent away empty. He has helped his servant Israel, in remembrance of his mercy, as he spoke to our fathers, to Abraham and to his offspring forever." — "If my people who are called by my name humble themselves, and pray and seek my face and turn from their wicked ways, then I will hear from heaven and will forgive their sin and heal their land." — But this is the one to whom I will look: he who is humble and contrite in spirit and trembles at my word. — He leads the humble in what is right, and teaches the humble his way.

Psa. 18:27. Deut. 8:2–3,16. Luke 1:51–55. 2 Chron. 7:14. Isa. 66:2. Psa. 25:9.

Humility

Day 14 Prayer

Thank you, Father, that you save a humble people, an afflicted people. Forty years you led your people in the wilderness that you might humble them, testing them to know what was in their heart, whether they would keep your commandments or not, feeding them with manna that you might humble them and test them, to do them good in the end. You brought down the mighty from their thrones and exalted those of humble estate, Israel, in remembrance of your mercy to Abraham and to his offspring forever. So if your people who are called by your name humble themselves, and pray and seek your face and turn from their wicked ways, then you will hear from heaven and will forgive their sin and heal their land. For you look to the one who is humble and contrite in spirit and trembles at your word. You lead the humble in what is right and teach the humble your way. You save a humble people. Bless you, Father.

Israel, My Servant

Day 15 Scriptures

But you, Israel, my servant, Jacob, whom I have chosen, the off-spring of Abraham, my friend; you whom I took from the ends of the earth, and called from its farthest corners, saying to you, "You are my servant, I have chosen you and not cast you off"; fear not, for I am with you; be not dismayed, for I am your God; I will strengthen you, I will help you, I will uphold you with my righteous right hand. — Remember these things, O Jacob, and Israel, for you are my servant; I formed you; you are my servant; O Israel, you will not be forgotten by me. I have blotted out your transgressions like a cloud and your sins like mist; return to me, for I have redeemed you. — "But now hear, O Jacob my servant, Israel whom I have chosen! Thus says the LORD who made you, who formed you from the womb and will help you: Fear not, O Jacob my servant, Jeshurun whom I have chosen. For I will pour water on the thirsty land, and streams on the dry ground; I will pour my Spirit upon your offspring, and my blessing on your descendants. — "Then fear not, O Jacob my servant, declares the LORD, nor be dismayed, O Israel; for behold, I will save you from far away, and your offspring from the land of their captivity. Jacob shall return and have quiet and ease, and none shall make him afraid. For I am with you and will save you," says the LORD. — Let those who delight in my righteousness shout for joy and be glad and say evermore, "Great is the LORD, who delights in the welfare of his servant!" — You have dealt well with your servant, O LORD, according to your word. Teach me good judgment and knowledge, for I believe in your commandments. Before I was afflicted I went astray, but now I keep your word. — He has helped his servant Israel, in remembrance of his mercy, as he spoke to our fathers, to Abraham and to his offspring forever."

Isa. 41:8–10. Isa. 44:21–22. Isa. 44:1–3. Jer 30:10–11.
Psa. 35:27. Psa. 119:65–67. Luke 1:54–55.

Israel, My Servant

Day 15 Prayer

Father, thank you that Israel is your servant whom you have chosen, the offspring of Abraham, your friend, whom you took from the ends of the earth, and called from its farthest corners, saying, "You are my servant; I have chosen you and not cast you off;" and to whom you say, "Fear not for I am with you, be not dismayed for I am your God, I will strengthen you, I will help you, I will uphold you with my righteous right hand." Israel your servant will not be forgotten by you, and you have blotted out their transgressions like a cloud, and their sins like a mist; they are to return to you, for you have redeemed them. Yes, Jacob your servant, Israel whom you have chosen, whom you made and formed from the womb and will help, is to fear not, for you will pour water on the thirsty land and streams on the dry ground; you will pour your Spirit upon their offspring and your blessing on their descendants. You will save Jacob your servant from far away, and their offspring from the land of their captivity; they shall return and have quiet and ease, and none shall make them afraid, for you are with them to save them. Indeed, you delight in the welfare of your servant, you have dealt well with your servant, you have helped your servant Israel, in remembrance of your mercy, as you spoke to their fathers, to Abraham and his offspring forever. Praise you Lord!

Israel, No Longer Ashamed

DAY 16 SCRIPTURES

To you, O Lord, I lift up my soul. O my God, in you I trust; let me not be put to shame; let not my enemies exult over me. Indeed, none who wait for you shall be put to shame. — Those who look to him are radiant, and their faces shall never be ashamed. — Therefore thus says the Lord, who redeemed Abraham, concerning the house of Jacob: "Jacob shall no more be ashamed, no more shall his face grow pale. For when he sees his children, the work of my hands in his midst, they will sanctify my name; they will sanctify the Holy One of Jacob and will stand in awe of the God of Israel." — "Therefore thus says the Lord God: Now I will restore the fortunes of Jacob and have mercy on the whole house of Israel, and I will be jealous for my holy name. They shall forget their shame and all the treachery they have practiced against me, when they dwell securely in their land with none to make them afraid, when I have brought them back from the peoples and gathered them from their enemies' lands." — "Behold, at that time I will deal with all your oppressors. And I will save the lame and gather the outcast, and I will change their shame into praise and renown in all the earth. At that time I will bring you in, at the time when I gather you together; for I will make you renowned and praised among all the peoples of the earth, when I restore your fortunes before your eyes," says the LORD. — "Fear not, for you will not be ashamed; be not confounded, for you will not be disgraced; for you will forget the shame of your youth . . . For a brief moment I deserted you, but with great compassion I will gather you. In overflowing anger for a moment I hid my face from you, but with everlasting love I will have compassion on you," says the Lord, your Redeemer." — Instead of your shame there shall be a double portion; instead of dishonor they shall rejoice in their lot.

PSA. 25:1–2; 34:5. ISA. 29:22–23. EZEK. 39:25–27.
ZEPH. 3:19–20. ISA. 54:4, 7–8. ISA. 61:7.

Israel, No Longer Ashamed
Day 16 Prayer

Thank you, Father, that none who wait for you shall be put to shame, that those who look to you are radiant and their faces shall never be ashamed. Thank you that Jacob shall no more be ashamed, no more shall his face grow pale; for when he sees his children, the work of your hands, in his midst, they will sanctify your name. Yes, you will restore the fortunes of Jacob and have mercy on the whole house of Israel, and they shall forget their shame and all the treachery they have practiced against you. Behold, at that time you will deal with all their oppressors; you will save the lame and gather the outcast and change their shame into praise and renown in all the earth when you restore their fortunes before their eyes. They will not be ashamed or disgraced and will forget the shame of their youth; though for a brief moment you deserted them, with great compassion you will gather them. Though in overflowing anger for a moment you hid your face from them, with everlasting love you will have compassion on them, O Lord, their Redeemer. Instead of their shame there shall be a double portion, and instead of dishonor they shall rejoice in their lot. Indeed, none who wait for you shall be put to shame. Bless you, Father!

Justice

DAY 17 SCRIPTURES

The LORD is exalted, for he dwells on high; he will fill Zion with justice and righteousness. — Justice is turned back, and righteousness stands far away . . . Truth is lacking . . . The LORD saw it, and it displeased him that there was no justice. — Why do you say, O Jacob, and speak, O Israel, "My way is hidden from the LORD, and my right is disregarded by my God"? — "Shall not the Judge of all the earth do what is just?" — For the LORD will not forsake his people; he will not abandon his heritage; for justice will return to the righteous, and all the upright in heart will follow it. — Righteousness and justice are the foundation of his throne. — "The Rock, his work is perfect, for all his ways are justice. A God of faithfulness and without iniquity, just and upright is he." — Zion shall be redeemed by justice, and those in her who repent, by righteousness. — Until the Spirit is poured upon us from on high . . . Then justice will dwell in the wilderness, and righteousness abide in the fruitful field. — For the LORD is a God of justice; blessed are all those who wait for him.

ISA. 33:5, 59:14–15, 40:27. GEN. 18:25. PSA. 94:14–15, 97:2, 103:6.
DEUT. 32:4. ISA.1:27, 32:15–16, 30:18.

Justice

Day 17 Prayer

Thank you, Father, that you will fill Zion with justice and righteousness. When justice is turned back, righteousness stands far away and truth is lacking, you see it and it displeases you that there is no justice. So why do you say, O Jacob, and speak O Israel, "My way is hidden from the Lord, and my right is disregarded by my God"? Shall not the Judge of all the earth do what is just? For you, O Lord, will not forsake your people, you will not abandon your heritage; for justice will return to the righteous and all the upright in heart will follow it. Righteousness and justice are the foundation of your throne; you work righteousness and justice for all who are oppressed. Your work is perfect, for all your ways are justice; a God of faithfulness and without iniquity, just and upright are you. Thank you that Zion shall be redeemed by justice, and those in her who repent, by righteousness. Thank you that when the Spirit is poured upon us from on high then justice will dwell in the wilderness, and righteousness abide in the fruitful field. For you are a God of justice; blessed are all those who wait for you. Thank you, Father.

Land — Patriarchs

Day 18 Scriptures

And the angel of the LORD called to Abraham . . . "I will surely bless you, and I will surely multiply your offspring as the stars of heaven . . . and in your offspring shall all the nations of the earth be blessed, because you have obeyed my voice." — The LORD said to Abram, after Lot had separated from him, "Lift up your eyes and look . . . for all the land that you see I will give to you and to your offspring forever." — And the LORD appeared to him [Isaac] and said, "Do not go down to Egypt; dwell in the land of which I shall tell you. Sojourn in this land, and I will be with you and will bless you, for to you and to your offspring I will give all these lands, and I will establish the oath that I swore to Abraham your father. I will multiply your offspring as the stars of heaven and will give to your offspring all these lands. And in your offspring all the nations of the earth shall be blessed." — And behold, the LORD stood beside him [Jacob] and said, "I am the LORD, the God of Abraham your father and the God of Isaac. The land on which you lie I will give to you and to your offspring . . . and in you and your offspring shall all the families of the earth be blessed." — But Moses implored the LORD his God and said . . ."Remember Abraham, Isaac, and Israel, your servants, to whom you swore by your own self, and said to them, 'I will multiply your offspring as the stars of heaven, and all this land that I have promised I will give to your offspring, and they shall inherit it forever.'" — He remembers his covenant forever, the word that he commanded, for a thousand generations, the covenant that he made with Abraham, his sworn promise to Isaac, which he confirmed to Jacob as a statute, to Israel as an everlasting covenant, saying, "To you I will give the land of Canaan as your portion for an inheritance."

Gen. 22:15,17,18; 13:14–15; 26:2–4. Gen. 28:12–14.
Ex. 32:11, 13. Psa. 105:8–11.

Land — Patriarchs

DAY 18 PRAYER

Father, you said to Abraham that you would surely bless him and multiply his offspring as the stars of heaven, and in his offspring all the families of the earth would be blessed, because he obeyed your voice. You said he should lift up his eyes and look, for all the land he saw you would give to him and his offspring forever. And you said to Isaac to sojourn in this land, and you would establish the oath you swore to Abraham his father; you would multiply his offspring as the stars of heaven and would give to his offspring all these lands, and in his offspring all the nations of the earth would be blessed. And to Jacob you said that the land on which he was lying you would give to his offspring, and in his offspring all the families of the earth would be blessed. Moses implored you to remember Abraham, Isaac, and Israel, your servants, to whom you swore by your own self that you would multiply their offspring as the stars of heaven, and that all the land you promised you would give to their offspring, who would inherit it forever. Thank you, Father, that you remember the word you commanded to a thousand generations, the everlasting covenant you made with Abraham, Isaac, and Jacob, saying that to them you would give the land of Canaan as their portion for an inheritance. For you remember your covenant forever. Bless you, Father.

The Lord's Right Hand

DAY 19 SCRIPTURES

But you, Israel, my servant . . . I will strengthen you, I will help you, I will uphold you with my righteous right hand. —You brought a vine out of Egypt; you drove out the nations and planted it . . . the stock that your right hand planted.—He brought them to his holy land, to the mountain which his right hand had won.—For not by their own sword did they win the land, nor did their own arm save them, but your right hand and your arm, and the light of your face, for you delighted in them.—As your name, O God, so your praise reaches to the ends of the earth. Your right hand is filled with righteousness. Let Mount Zion be glad!—You have set up a banner for those who fear you, that they may flee to it from the bow. That your beloved ones may be delivered, give salvation by your right hand.— In your majesty ride forth victoriously in the cause of truth, humility and justice; let your right hand achieve awesome deeds.— Sing to the LORD a new song, for he performs amazing deeds! His right hand and his mighty arm accomplish deliverance.— Shouts of joy and victory resound in the tents of the righteous: "The LORD'S right hand has done mighty things! The LORD'S right hand is lifted high!"

ISA. 41:8,10. PSA. 80:8, 15, 78:54, 44:3, 48:10–11,
60:4–5, 45:4 (NIV), 98:1 (NET), PSA. 118:15–16 (NIV).

The Lord's Right Hand

Day 19 Prayer

Thank you, Father, that you will strengthen, you will help, you will uphold Israel with your righteous right hand. You brought a vine out of Egypt: you drove out the nations and planted it with your right hand. You brought them to your holy land, to the mountain which your right hand had won. For not by their own sword did they win the land, nor did their own arm save them, but your right hand and your arm, and the light of your face, for you delighted in them. As your name, O God, so your praise reaches to the ends of the earth; your right hand is filled with righteousness. Let Mount Zion be glad! You have set up a banner for those who fear you that they may flee to it from the bow. That your beloved ones may be delivered, give salvation by your right hand. In your majesty ride forth victoriously in the cause of truth, humility and justice; let your right hand achieve awesome deeds. Yes, you perform amazing deeds! Your right hand and your mighty arm accomplish deliverance. Shouts of joy and victory resound in the tents of the righteous because your right hand has done mighty things, your right hand is lifted high! Hallelujah!

Not Forgotten/Not Forsaken

Day 20 Scriptures

For the Lord will not forsake his people; he will not abandon his heritage.—But Zion said, "The Lord has forsaken me; my Lord has forgotten me." Can a woman forget her nursing child, that she should have no compassion on the son of her womb? Even these may forget, yet I will not forget you."—For the mountains may depart and the hills be removed, but my steadfast love shall not depart from you, and my covenant of peace shall not be removed," says the Lord who has compassion on you.—When they are in the land of their enemies, I will not spurn them, neither will I abhor them so as to destroy them utterly and break my covenant with them, for I am the Lord their God.—For the Lord will not forsake his people, for his great name's sake, because it has pleased the Lord to make you a people for himself.—In the latter days you will return to the Lord your God and obey his voice. For the Lord your God is a merciful God. He will not leave you or destroy you or forget the covenant with your fathers that he swore to them.—God has not rejected his people whom he foreknew.—And they shall be called The Holy People, The Redeemed of the Lord; and you shall be called Sought Out, A City Not Forsaken.

Psa. 94:14. Isa. 49:14–15. Isa. 54:10. Lev. 26:44. 1 Sam. 12:22.
Deut. 4:30–31. Rom. 11:2. Isa. 62:12.

Not Forgotten/Not Forsaken

Day 20 Prayer

Thank you, Father, that you will not forsake your people; you will not abandon your heritage. Even if a woman could forget her nursing child that she should have no compassion on the son of her womb, you will not forget Zion. For the mountains may depart and the hills be removed, but your steadfast love shall not depart from them and your covenant of peace shall not be removed, for you are the Lord who has compassion on them. When they are in the land of their enemies, you will not spurn them, neither will you abhor them so as to destroy them utterly and break your covenant with them. For you will not forsake your people for your great name's sake, because it has pleased you to make them a people for yourself. Indeed, in the latter days they will return to you and obey your voice, for you are a merciful God, and will not leave or destroy them, or forget the covenant that you swore to their fathers. Yes, you have not rejected your people whom you foreknew. They shall be called The Holy People, The Redeemed of the Lord; and Zion shall be called Sought Out, A City Not Forsaken.

Peace of Jerusalem

Day 21 Scriptures

"Then fear not, O Jacob my servant, declares the LORD, nor be dismayed, O Israel . . . For I am with you to save you, declares the LORD." — Behold, I will bring to it [Jerusalem] health and healing, and I will heal them and reveal to them abundance of prosperity and security. — "I will make with them a covenant of peace . . . They shall dwell securely, and none shall make them afraid." — If it had not been the LORD who was on our side when people rose up against us, then they would have swallowed us up alive . . . the flood would have swept us away . . . Blessed be the LORD, who has not given us as prey to their teeth! We have escaped like a bird from the snare of the fowlers . . . Our help is in the name of the LORD, who made heaven and earth. — He will not let your foot be moved; he who keeps you will not slumber. Behold, he who keeps Israel will neither slumber nor sleep. — Pray for the peace of Jerusalem! "May they be secure who love you! Peace be within your walls and security within your towers!" — And when he [Jesus] drew near and saw the city [Jerusalem], he wept over it, saying, "Would that you, even you, had known on this day the things that make for peace! — For to us a child is born, to us a son is given; and the government shall be upon his shoulder, and his name shall be called Wonderful Counselor, Mighty God, Everlasting Father, Prince of Peace.

Jer. 30:10–11, 33:6. Ezek. 34:25,28. Psa. 124:2–4,6–8, 121:3–4, 122:6–8. Luke 19:41–42. Isa. 9:6.

Peace of Jerusalem

Day 21 Prayer

Thank you, Father, that Jacob is not to fear, Israel is not to be dismayed; for you are with them to save them. Thank you that you will bring to Jerusalem health and healing and reveal to them abundance of prosperity and security. You will make with them a covenant of peace; they shall dwell securely, and none shall make them afraid. Yes, if you had not been on their side, they would have been swallowed up alive, the flood would have swept them away. But you have not given them as prey to their teeth; they have escaped like a bird from the snare of the fowler. Their help is in you who made heaven and earth. You will not let their foot be moved; behold you who keep Israel will neither slumber nor sleep.

We pray for your peace, O Jerusalem! Peace be within your walls and security within your towers. May you know the things that make for peace. May you know the child born to you, the son given to you; on whose shoulder shall be the government, and whose name is called Wonderful Counselor, Mighty God, Everlasting Father, Prince of Peace.

Provision

Day 22 Scriptures

For the LORD has chosen Zion; he has desired it for his dwelling place: "This is my resting place forever; here I will dwell, for I have desired it. I will abundantly bless her provisions; I will satisfy her poor with bread." — The LORD has sworn by his right hand and by his mighty arm: "I will not again give your grain to be food for your enemies, and foreigners shall not drink your wine for which you have labored; but those who garner it shall eat it and praise the LORD, and those who gather it shall drink it in the courts of my sanctuary." — Yes, the LORD will give what is good, and our land will yield its increase. — You crown the year with your bounty; your wagon tracks overflow with abundance. The pastures of the wilderness overflow, the hills gird themselves with joy, the meadows clothe themselves with flocks, the valleys deck themselves with grain, they shout and sing together for joy. — And my God will supply every need of yours according to his riches in glory in Christ Jesus. — The earth has yielded its increase; God, our God, shall bless us. God shall bless us; let all the ends of the earth fear him!

Psa. 132:13–15. Isa. 62: 8–9. Psa. 85:12, 65:11–13. Phil 4:19. Psa. 67:7–8.

Provision

DAY 22 PRAYER

Thank you, Father, that you have chosen Zion; you have desired it for your resting place forever, and you will abundantly bless her provisions and will satisfy her poor with bread. We pray that you would not again give her grain to be food for her enemies, and foreigners would not drink her wine for which she has labored; but that those who garner it would eat it and praise the Lord, and those who gather it would drink it in the courts of your sanctuary. Yes, you will give what is good and her land will yield its increase. You crown the year with your bounty; the wagon tracks overflow with abundance. The pastures of the wilderness overflow, the hills gird themselves with joy, the meadows clothe themselves with flocks, the valleys deck themselves with grain; they shout and sing together for joy. For you will supply every need according to your riches in glory in Christ Jesus. The earth has yielded its increase; you shall bless them and let all the ends of the earth fear you!

Rebuilding

Day 23 Scriptures

I will restore the fortunes of my people Israel, and they shall rebuild the ruined cities and inhabit them; they shall plant vineyards and drink their wine, and they shall make gardens and eat their fruit. — They shall build up the ancient ruins; they shall raise up the former devastations; they shall repair the ruined cities, the devastations of many generations. — "In that day I will raise up the booth of David that is fallen and repair its breaches, and raise up its ruins and rebuild it as in the days of old." — And your ancient ruins shall be rebuilt; you shall raise up the foundations of many generations; you shall be called the repairer of the breach, the restorer of streets to dwell in. — Foreigners shall build up your walls, and their kings shall minister to you. — Again I will build you, and you shall be built, O virgin Israel! Again, you shall adorn yourself with tambourines and shall go forth in the dance of the merrymakers. Again you shall plant vineyards on the mountains of Samaria; the planters shall plant and shall enjoy the fruit. — I will restore the fortunes of Judah and the fortunes of Israel, and rebuild them as they were at first.

Amos 9:14. Isa. 61:4. Amos 9:11. Isa. 58:12; 60:10. Jer. 31:4–5, 33:7.

Rebuilding

Day 23 Prayer

Thank you, Father, that you will restore the fortunes of your people Israel, and they shall rebuild the ruined cities and inhabit them. They shall build up the ancient ruins; they shall raise up the former devastations; they shall repair the ruined cities, the devastations of many generations. And in that day you will raise up the booth of David that is fallen and repair its breaches, and raise up its ruins and rebuild it as in the days of old. Yes, their ancient ruins shall be rebuilt; they shall raise up the foundations of many generations and shall be called the repairer of the breach, the restorer of streets to dwell in. Indeed, foreigners shall build up the walls, and their kings shall minister to them.

O Israel, again the Lord will build you and you shall be rebuilt. Again, you shall adorn yourself with tambourines and shall go forth in the dance of the merrymakers. Again, you shall plant vineyards on the mountains of Samaria; the planters shall plant and shall enjoy the fruit.

For you, Father, will restore the fortunes of Judah and the fortunes of Israel, and rebuild them as they were at first. Bless you, Father.

Rejoice with Jerusalem

DAY 24 SCRIPTURES

But be glad and rejoice forever in that which I create; for behold, I create Jerusalem to be a joy, and her people to be a gladness. I will rejoice in Jerusalem and be glad in my people; no more shall be heard in it the sound of weeping and the cry of distress. — For as a young man marries a young woman, so shall your sons marry you, and as the bridegroom rejoices over the bride, so shall your God rejoice over you. — On that day it shall be said to Jerusalem: "Fear not, O Zion; let not your hands grow weak. The LORD your God is in your midst, a mighty one who will save; he will rejoice over you with gladness; he will quiet you by his love; he will exult over you with loud singing." — I will make with them an everlasting covenant, that I will not turn away from doing good to them. And I will put the fear of me in their hearts, that they may not turn from me. I will rejoice in doing them good, and I will plant them in this land in faithfulness, with all my heart and all my soul. — To grant to those who mourn in Zion, to give them a beautiful headdress instead of ashes, the oil of gladness instead of mourning, the garment of praise instead of a faint spirit. — Break forth together into singing, you waste places of Jerusalem, for the LORD has comforted his people; he has redeemed Jerusalem. — "Rejoice with Jerusalem, and be glad for her, all you who love her; rejoice with her in joy, all you who mourn over her."

ISA. 65:18–19; 62:5. ZEPH. 3:16–17. JER. 32:40–41. ISA. 61:3; 52:9–10; 66:10.

Rejoice with Jerusalem

Day 24 Prayer

Father, we will be glad and rejoice forever in that which you create; for, behold, you create Jerusalem to be a joy, and her people to be a gladness. You will rejoice in Jerusalem and be glad in your people. As the bridegroom rejoices over the bride, so shall you rejoice over her. For you are in her midst, a mighty one who will save; you will rejoice over her with gladness; you will quiet her by your love; you will exult over her with loud singing. We thank you for your everlasting covenant that you will not turn away from doing good to her; you will put the fear of you in their hearts that they may not turn from you; and you will rejoice in doing them good and will plant them in this land in faithfulness, with all your heart and all your soul. You will grant to those who mourn in Zion a beautiful headdress instead of ashes, the oil of gladness instead of mourning, the garment of praise instead of a faint spirit. The waste places of Jerusalem break forth together into singing, for you have comforted your people, you have redeemed Jerusalem. We rejoice with Jerusalem and are glad for her, all we who love her; we rejoice with her in joy. For you have created her to be a joy, and her people to be a gladness. Thank you, Father!

Remember, Recount

Day 25 Scriptures

I will recount the steadfast love of the LORD, the praises of the LORD, according to all that the LORD has granted us, and the great goodness to the house of Israel that he has granted them according to his compassion, according to the abundance of his steadfast love. — Praise the LORD! Oh give thanks to the LORD, for he is good, for his steadfast love endures forever! Who can utter the mighty deeds of the LORD, or declare all his praise? — I will remember the deeds of the LORD; yes, I will remember your wonders of old. I will ponder all your work, and meditate on your mighty deeds. Your way, O God, is holy. What god is great like our God? You are the God who works wonders; you have made known your might among the peoples. You with your arm redeemed your people, the children of Jacob and Joseph. — Remember the wondrous works that he has done, his miracles and the judgments he uttered, O offspring of Israel his servant, children of Jacob, his chosen ones! — But we your people, the sheep of your pasture, will give thanks to you forever; from generation to generation we will recount your praise. — Great are the works of the LORD, studied by all who delight in them. Full of splendor and majesty is his work, and his righteousness endures forever. He has caused his wondrous works to be remembered; the LORD is gracious and merciful.

Isa. 63:7. Psa. 106:1–2, 77:11–15. 1 Chron. 16:12–13. Psa. 79:13, 111:2–4.

Remember, Recount

Day 25 Prayer

Father, we recount your steadfast love and your great goodness to the house of Israel, according to all you have granted to them, according to the abundance of your steadfast love. We give thanks to you, O Lord, for you are good and your love endures forever. Who can utter your mighty deeds or declare all your praise? We remember your deeds; yes, we remember your wonders of old. We ponder all your work and meditate on your mighty deeds. Your way, O God, is holy, working wonders, making known your might among the peoples, and with your arm redeeming your people, the children of Jacob and Joseph. Let the offspring of Abraham, your servant, the children of Jacob, your chosen ones, remember the wondrous works that you have done, your miracles and the judgments you uttered. From generation to generation may they recount your praise. For great are your works, O Lord, full of splendor and majesty. You have caused them to be remembered. Praise you, Lord!

Restoration

Day 26 Scriptures

For I will restore health to you, and your wounds I will heal, declares the Lord, because they have called you an outcast: 'It is Zion, for whom no one cares!' "Thus says the LORD: Behold, I will restore the fortunes of the tents of Jacob and have compassion on his dwellings." — "Therefore thus says the Lord God: Now I will restore the fortunes of Jacob and have mercy on the whole house of Israel, and I will be jealous for my holy name. — "I will restore the fortunes of my people Israel, and they shall rebuild the ruined cities and inhabit them; they shall plant vineyards and drink their wine, and they shall make gardens and eat their fruit. I will plant them on their land, and they shall never again be uprooted out of the land that I have given them," says the Lord your God. — I will restore Israel to his pasture, and he shall feed on Carmel and in Bashan, and his desire shall be satisfied on the hill of Ephraim and in Gilead. — Lord, you were favorable to your land; you restored the fortunes of Jacob. You forgave the iniquity of your people; you covered all their sin. — Oh, that salvation for Israel would come out of Zion! When the Lord restores the fortunes of his people, let Jacob rejoice, let Israel be glad. — When the Lord restored the fortunes of Zion, we were like those who dream. Then our mouth was filled with laughter, and our tongue with shouts of joy; then they said among the nations, "The Lord has done great things for them."

Jer 30:17–18. Ezek. 39:25. Amos 9:14–15. Jer. 50:19. Psa. 85:1–2; 14:7, 126:1–2

Restoration

Day 26 Prayer

Thank you, Father, that you will restore the fortunes of the tents of Jacob and have compassion on his dwellings; you will restore health to them and their wounds you will heal. Yes, you will restore the fortunes of Jacob and have mercy on the whole house of Israel and will be jealous for your holy name. You will restore the fortunes of Israel and they shall rebuild the ruined cities and inhabit them; they shall plant vineyards and drink their wine and they shall make gardens and eat their fruit. You will plant them on their land, and they shall never again be uprooted out of the land that you have given them. You will restore Israel to his pasture, and he shall feed on Carmel and in Bashan, and his desire shall be satisfied on the hill of Ephraim and in Gilead. Lord you were favorable to your land; you restored the fortunes of Jacob, forgiving the iniquity of your people and covering their sin. Oh, that salvation for Israel would come out of Zion! When you restore the fortunes of your people, let Jacob rejoice, let Israel be glad! And let them say among the nations that you have done great things for them! Hallelujah!

Righteousness

Day 27 Scriptures

Christ Jesus, who became to us wisdom from God, righteousness and sanctification and redemption. — For, being ignorant of the righteousness of God, and seeking to establish their own, they did not submit to God's righteousness. For Christ is the end of the law for righteousness to everyone who believes. — And he [Abraham] believed the LORD, and he counted it to him as righteousness. — You shall be called the city of righteousness, the faithful city. Zion shall be redeemed by justice, and those in her who repent, by righteousness. — For Zion's sake I will not keep silent, and for Jerusalem's sake I will not be quiet, until her righteousness goes forth as brightness, and her salvation as a burning torch. The nations shall see your righteousness, and all the kings your glory. — The Lord has made known his salvation; he has revealed his righteousness in the sight of the nations. He has remembered his steadfast love and faithfulness to the house of Israel.

1 Cor. 1: 30. Rom. 10: 3–4. Gen. 15:6. Isa. 1:26–27; 62:1–2. Psa. 98:2–3.

Righteousness

Day 27 Prayer

Thank you, Father, for Jesus whom you have made our wisdom and our righteousness and sanctification and redemption. Thank you that he is the end of the law for righteousness to everyone who believes. Thank you for Abraham who believed you and you counted it to him as righteousness. Thank you that Zion shall be called the city of righteousness, the faithful city; she shall be redeemed by justice, and those in her who repent, by righteousness. So for Zion's sake we will not keep silent, and for Jerusalem's sake we will not be quiet, until her righteousness goes forth as brightness, and her salvation as a burning torch; the nations shall see your righteousness, and all the kings your glory. Yes, Father, you have made known your salvation; you have revealed your righteousness in the sight of the nations. You have remembered your steadfast love and faithfulness to the house of Israel. Praise you, Lord!

Shalom

Day 28 Scriptures

Pray for the peace of Jerusalem! May they be secure who love you! — For I know the plans I have for you, declares the Lord, plans for wholeness and not for evil, to give you a future and a hope. — If you will walk in my statutes and observe my commandments and do them, then . . . I will give peace in the land, and you shall lie down, and none shall make you afraid. — The Lord spoke to Moses, saying, "Speak to Aaron and his sons, saying, Thus you shall bless the people of Israel: you shall say to them, The Lord bless you and keep you; the Lord make his face to shine upon you and be gracious to you; the Lord lift up his countenance upon you and give you peace." — For thus says the Lord: "Behold, I will extend peace to her like a river . . . As one whom his mother comforts, so I will comfort you; you shall be comforted in Jerusalem." — My people will abide in a peaceful habitation, in secure dwellings, and in quiet resting places. — Let me hear what God the Lord will speak, for he will speak peace to his people, to his saints; but let them not turn back to folly. — "For the mountains may depart and the hills be removed, but my steadfast love shall not depart from you, and my covenant of peace shall not be removed," says the Lord, who has compassion on you. — And his name shall be called Wonderful Counselor, Mighty God, Everlasting Father, Prince of Peace. Of the increase of his government and of peace there will be no end.

Psa. 122:6. Jer. 29:11. Lev. 26:3,6. Num. 6:22–26. Isa. 66:12, 13; 32:18. Psa. 85:8. Isa. 54:10; 9:6–7

Shalom

DAY 28 PRAYER

Father, we pray for the peace of Jerusalem; may they be secure who love her! Your plans for her are for wholeness and not for evil, to give her a future and a hope. You have said that if they would walk in your statutes and observe your commandments and do them, you will give peace in the land, and they shall lie down and none shall make them afraid. You will bless them, keep them, make your face to shine upon them and be gracious to them, lift up your countenance upon them and give them peace. You will extend peace to Jerusalem like a river; as one whom his mother comforts, so you will comfort them; they shall be comforted in Jerusalem. Your people will abide in a peaceful habitation, in secure dwellings, and in quiet resting places. Yes, you will speak peace to your people, but let them not turn back to folly. Indeed, the mountains may depart and the hills be removed, but your steadfast love shall not depart from them and your covenant of peace shall not be removed. For Jesus is the Wonderful Counselor, Mighty God, Everlasting Father, Prince of Peace, of the increase of whose government and of peace there will be no end. Hallelujah!

Shepherd — Aliyah[*]

DAY 29 SCRIPTURES

He will tend his flock like a shepherd; he will gather the lambs in his arms; he will carry them in his bosom, and gently lead those that are with young. — Oh, save your people and bless your heritage! Be their shepherd and carry them forever. — Give ear, O Shepherd of Israel, you who lead Joseph like a flock! You who are enthroned upon the cherubim, shine forth. Before Ephraim and Benjamin and Manasseh, stir up your might and come to save us! — "Hear the word of the LORD, O nations, and declare it in the coastlands far away; say, 'He who scattered Israel will gather him, and will keep him as a shepherd keeps his flock.' — "My sheep were scattered over all the face of the earth, with none to search or seek for them . . . .They were scattered, because there was no shepherd . . . Thus says the Lord GOD: Behold, I, I myself will search for my sheep and will seek them out. As a shepherd seeks out his flock . . . so will I seek out my sheep . . . And I will bring them out from the peoples and gather them from the countries, and will bring them into their own land. And I will feed them on the mountains of Israel . . . There they shall lie down in good grazing land, and on rich pasture they shall feed on the mountains of Israel. I myself will be the shepherd of my sheep."

ISA. 40:11. PSA. 28:9; 80:1–2. JER. 31:10. EZEK. 34:5,6,11–15.

---

[*] "Aliyah" means "to go up," and signifies the return of the Jewish people from the Diaspora to the land of Israel.

Shepherd — Aliyah
Day 29 Prayer

Thank you, Father, that you will tend your flock like a shepherd; you will gather the lambs in your arms; you will carry them in your bosom, and gently lead those that are with young. You will save your people and bless your heritage; you will be their Shepherd and carry them forever. So, give ear O Shepherd of Israel, you who lead Joseph like a flock, stir up your might and come to save them! For you who scattered Israel will gather him and will keep him as a shepherd keeps his flock. Your sheep were scattered over all the face of the earth, but you yourself will search for your sheep and seek them out. As a shepherd seeks out his flock, so you will seek out your sheep. You will bring them out from the peoples and gather them from the countries, and you will bring them into their own land. You will feed them on the mountains of Israel where they shall lie down in good grazing land, and on rich pasture they shall feed. And you, yourself, will be the shepherd of your sheep. Thank you, Father.

The Spirit

Day 30 Scriptures

"And it shall come to pass afterward, that I will pour out my Spirit on all flesh; your sons and your daughters shall prophesy, your old men shall dream dreams, and your young men shall see visions." — "And I will not hide my face anymore from them, when I pour out my Spirit upon the house of Israel, declares the Lord GOD." — "You stiff-necked people . . . you always resist the Holy Spirit. As your fathers did, so do you." — "And I will pour out on the house of David and the inhabitants of Jerusalem a spirit of grace and supplication." — "Prophesy to the breath; prophesy, son of man, and say to the breath, Thus says the Lord GOD: Come from the four winds, O breath, and breathe on these slain, that they may live." So I prophesied as he commanded me, and the breath came into them, and they lived and stood on their feet, an exceedingly great army. . . . "And I will put my Spirit within you, and you shall live, and I will place you in your own land. Then you shall know that I am the LORD." — Until the Spirit is poured upon us from on high, and the wilderness becomes a fruitful field, and the fruitful field is deemed a forest. Then justice will dwell in the wilderness, and righteousness abide in the fruitful field. And the effect of righteousness will be peace, and the result of righteousness, quietness and trust forever. My people will abide in a peaceful habitation, in secure dwellings, and in quiet resting places.

Joel 2:28. Ezek. 39:29. Acts 7:51. Zech. 12:10 (NIV).
Ezek. 37:9–10, 14. Isa. 32:15–18.

The Spirit

Day 30 Prayer

Thank you, Father, that you will pour out your Spirit on all flesh; sons and daughters shall prophesy, old men shall dream dreams, and young men shall see visions. You will not hide your face anymore from them, when you pour out your Spirit upon the house of Israel. Though a stiff-necked people, resisting the Holy Spirit, as their fathers did, you will pour out on the house of David and the inhabitants of Jerusalem a spirit of grace and supplication. So, we prophecy to the breath, and say to the breath to come from the four winds and breathe on these slain that they may live and stand on their feet, an exceedingly great army. For you, Lord, will put your Spirit within them and they shall live; and you will place them in their own land; then they shall know that you are the Lord. Yes, when the Spirit is poured upon them from on high, the wilderness becomes a fruitful field, and the fruitful field is deemed a forest; then justice will dwell in the wilderness, and righteousness abide in the fruitful field. And the effect of righteousness will be peace, and your people will abide in a peaceful habitation, in secure dwellings, and in quiet resting places. Thank you, Father!

Waiting

Day 31 Scriptures

From of old no one has heard, or perceived by the ear, no eye has seen a God besides you, who acts for those who wait for him. — Why do you say, O Jacob, and speak, O Israel, "My way is hidden from the LORD, and my right is disregarded by my God"? Have you not known? Have you not heard? The LORD is the everlasting God, the Creator of the ends of the earth. He does not faint or grow weary; his understanding is unsearchable. He gives power to the faint, and to him who has no might he increases strength. Even youths shall faint and be weary, and young men shall fall exhausted; but they who wait for the LORD shall renew their strength; they shall mount up with wings like eagles; they shall run and not be weary; they shall walk and not faint. — I wait for the LORD, my soul waits, and in his word I hope; my soul waits for the Lord more than watchman for the morning, more than watchmen for the morning. O Israel, hope in the LORD! For with the LORD there is steadfast love, and with him is plentiful redemption. And he will redeem Israel from all his iniquities. — Wait for the LORD and keep his way, and he will exalt you to inherit the land; you will look on when the wicked are cut off. — Our soul waits for the LORD; he is our help and our shield. For our heart is glad in him, because we trust in his holy name. Let your steadfast love, O LORD, be upon us, even as we hope in you.

Isa. 64:4; 40:27–31. Psa. 130:5–8; 37:34; 27:14; 33:20–22.

Waiting

Day 31 Prayer

Thank you, Father, that from of old no one has heard or perceived by the ear, no eye has seen a God besides you who acts for those who wait for you.

So why do you say, O Jacob, and speak, O Israel, "My way is hidden from the Lord and my right is disregarded by my God?" Have you not known? Have you not heard? The Lord is the everlasting God, the creator of the ends of the earth; he does not faint or grow weary; his understanding is unsearchable. He gives power to the faint, and to him who has no might he increases strength. Even youths shall faint and be weary, and young men shall fall exhausted; but they who wait for him shall renew their strength; they shall mount up with wings like eagles; they shall run and not be weary; they shall walk and not faint. O Israel, hope in the Lord! For with the Lord there is steadfast love, and with him is plentiful redemption, and he will redeem you from all your iniquities. Wait for the Lord and keep his way, and he will exalt you to inherit the land; you will look on when the wicked are cut off. Wait for the Lord and let your heart take courage; wait for the Lord!

So, Father, may Israel wait for you, you are their help and their shield. May their hearts be glad in you because they trust in your holy name. Let your steadfast love, O Lord, be upon them even as they hope in you. Bless you, Father!

Scripture References

Genesis
12:1,3 Day 1
13:14–15 Day 18
15:6 Day 27
18:25 Day 17
22:15,17,18 Day 18
22:18 Day 1
26:2–4 Day 18
28:12–14 Day 18

Exodus
18:8–9 Day 13
29:45–46 Day 10
32:11,13 Day 18

Leviticus
23:3,6 Day 28

Numbers
6:22–26 Day 28
35:34 Day 10

Deuteronomy
4:37–38 Day 6
7:6–8 Day 6
8: 2–3, 16 Day 14
10:14–15 Day 6
32:9–10 Days 2, 5
32:14 Day 17

Joshua
21:45 Day 12

1 Samuel
12:22 Day 5

1 Chronicles
16:12–13 Day 25
23:25 Day 10

2 Chronicles
7:14 Days 11, 14
20:17 Day 9

Nehemiah
9:7 Day 6
9:17 Day 11
9:25 Day 13

Psalm
9:19 Day 4
10:12 Day 4
12:5 Day 4
14:7 Day 26
17:8–9 Day 2
18:19 Day 5
18:27 Day 14
25:1–2 Day 16
25:9 Day 14
27:14 Day 31
28:9 Day 29
32:7 Day 9
33:18–19 Day 9
33:20–22 Day 31
34:5 Day 16
35:27 Day 15
36:5 Day 12
37:24 Day 31
50:15 Day 9
65:11–13 Day 22
67:1–2 Day 3
67:2–4 Day 1
67:7–8 Day 22
72:12 Day 9
73:1 Day 13
76:1–2 Day 10
79: 13 Day 25
80:1–2 Day 29
82:8 Day 4
85:1–2 Day 26
85:8 Day 28
85:12 Day 22
86:15 Day 12

Scripture References

Scripture References

Jeremiah
29:11 Day 28
30:10–11 Day 21
30:10–12 Day 15
30:17 Day 17
31:2–3 Day 5
31:4–5 Day 23
31:10 Day 29
31:10, 12, 13 Day 8
31:31, 33,34 Day 11
31:35–36 Day 12
32:40–41 Days 13, 24
33:6 Day 21
33:7–8 Days 7, 23
33:8 Day 11
33:9 Day 13
50:19 Days 11, 23

Ezekiel
34:5, 6, 11–15 Day 29
34:25, 28 Day 21
36:24–25 Day 7
37:9–10, 14 Day 30
37:27–28 Day 10
39:25 Day 26
39:25–27 Day 16
39:29 Day 30

Daniel
9:9 Day 11

Joel
2:28 Day 30
3:17, 21 Day 10

Amos
9:11, 14 Day 23
9:14–15 Day 26

Zephaniah
3:16–17 Day 24
3:19–20 Day 16

Zechariah
1:17 Day 8
2:8–9 Day 2
8:3–5 Day 10
8:7–8 Day 12
12:10 Days 7, 30

Matthew
24:14 Day 1

Luke
1:51–55 Day 14
1:54–55 Day 15
19:41–42 Day 21
21:33 Day 12

Acts
7:51 Day 30

Romans
10:3–4 Day 27
11:1 Day 5
11:5 Day 6
11:25 Day 1
11: 26 Day 9
11:25–27 Day 11
11:28–29 Day 5
11:29 Day 10

1 Corinthians
1:30 Day 27

Philippians
4:19 Day 22

1 John
1:9 Day 7

Revelation
7:9 Day 1

Appendix:
Listening Prayer Impressions

Here my wife, Kim, added her impressions of **God's response** to these prayers, day by day. Her practice was to appreciate his character revealed in these passages, pray these prayers, and and then pause to listen for his rhema word response to her heart. These impressions brought her peace and are included here simply as a model to inspire your own personal reflections and individual times of listening — as you interact with him on these themes so close to his heart.

All the Earth Blessed – Day 1

Real connection with me always creates a ripple effect. Others are always impacted by those who — like Abraham — respond to and are transformed by me. I rejoice in allowing people to help me reach people; in family transformation igniting other families — until all the families of the earth have opportunity to become part of my family, and so to experience my joy, shalom and blessing — together.

Apple of His Eye – Day 2

My people are the center of my care, my attention, my focus. I am so close, so present, so connected — whether they are aware, or not. I give people the freedom to direct their own attention, but also my good instruction (torah) as to how to best do that. I also allow challenges to these instructions — and challenges for my people, too. All under my careful oversight. I am a good Father, you see.

Appointed Time to Favor – Day 3

Thank you for joining me, for seeing my heart for my people, my children — how attentive I am to their cries for help, how I long to embrace and help and be with them. How I wait for them to invite me in, to welcome my presence. I have deep, heartfelt compassion and desire to nurture them. Do pray that they might see my heart, and open theirs to me. For it is high time, and I have so much to give.

Arise – Day 4

Like the rising sun, I arise over and over again upon Jerusalem and upon my people. I see, I hear, I feel their pain. I am with them, and I am strong to rescue them. Thank you for seeing who I am, for knowing my heart, and for joining me in this work. As my people come to know me as I truly am — the one who lifted myself up on their behalf — they will reflect my glory in a dark world more and more. And the nations will be drawn to this light. This is the desire of my heart, and my glorious plan.

Beloved – Day 5

I am the God who sees people rightly, truly, lovingly. I see the ones I have made, and called, and destined. My faithful, loving, delighting and transforming gaze rests upon them and draws them. My love is not based on their performance. It is rooted securely in *my* heart. *I* will bear the cost of my passionate pursuit of intimate relationship with my beloved people. It is so worth it to me.

Chosen – Day 6

My choices, my selections, of the people who I'd like to be specially mine are not made based on human perceptions of qualification — including their responsiveness to me. My love for people is not based on human factors at all. And my love never fails — it never rejects *persons* as they were created to be. It is always there for my loved ones. I am present and looking to them and helping them, though they and all the world may fail to perceive that. But thank you for joining me in praying my will, which is that the ones I choose will perceive and receive my invitation to loving connection, and know themselves to be special and chosen.

Cleansing – Day 7

Just as a good parent does not turn from embracing their dirty child who is in need of love, so I accept my people. I suffer the consequences in the process, but I am well able to handle the clean-up. I never lose the baby with the bathwater. The *child* is my pride and joy, and our relationship is foremost in my priorities.

Comfort – Day 8

As a father and a mother comforts their children, so I comfort mine. When all seems lost — conflicts within, conflicts without — I am gladly and tenderly present to see and to soothe and to restore courage and hope. I can help! My comforting presence helps my people return to joy; to knowing they belong with and to me and one another, and that my faithful love can restore shalom and fruitfulness.

Deliverance – Day 9

I have delivered, I will deliver, I am Deliverer. I hear the call of my people, I pluck them out of the enemy snares — I am hovering and watching, waiting for the "just right" moment. Like a child who knows that Daddy will catch him just in the nick of time, so my people can face their enemies — including death — with confident hope in me, who triumphs over them all.

Dwell – Day 10

I so desire to live among my people. To be welcomed into the midst of their daily lives, their homes, their streets, their work — not just their religious duties. Though I desire to dwell with them in the midst of those as well! Join me in yearning for the day when this is fully realized and I am fully welcomed with my transforming, redeeming Presence. Not just to visit, but to *dwell*.

Forgiveness – Day 11

Yes, I welcome my people to look me in the face. To come to me unguarded, honestly — needing help, needing cleansing, needing a new identity. In the light of my love, they (and you) are transformed, the *real* persons are seen, and we become deeply bonded together in covenant love. This result is what motivated my sacrifice. This is my joy.

God Faithful to His Word – Day 12

My faithfulness is something that can sometimes be hard to see — if you are looking at one small moment or happening. Seeing faithfulness calls for a wide-angle lens — at least for the novice. It calls for reading all the way to the end of a story, oftentimes. I *enjoy* inserting elements such as last minute shame/honor reversals, reconciliations, fulfillments of foreshadowing in unexpected ways, and the like. I am faithful. Look wide, and long, and you will see it. And grow in trust.

Goodness – Day 13

It is good for you to see, to know, to taste, and to savor my goodness. It opens up your mind and heart to perceive it so much more deeply. To receive it. To enjoy and notice the many signs of my goodness that I sometimes hide a bit — like treasures to reward the sharp-eyed seekers. Your perception of my goodness will grow the more you acknowledge it. And that is a good thing for you, and all my people. It's a delight, therefore, for me, too — as we enjoy one another's enjoyment.

Humility – Day 14

Afflictions happen in this world. I know it is hard to realize that I allow this. For Israel, for you, for others. It takes time and maturity to begin to see that I, too, experience affliction. Also that it is usually the afflicted, humbled and needy ones who open their hearts to me, my presence in the midst, and my redeeming power. The humble see my ability to bring good in the end. Look at my Son, and see this, and fear not — only draw near. I will feed you with manna that the proud, mighty and full will never know. And you will become bonded to me as my beloved children.

Israel, My Servant – Day 15

Those who help me in my work are my specially selected servants, subjects and worshippers. Not all are able to see the privilege that this is — to be chosen for the most elite and intimate and, yes, challenging and fulfilling mission and purposes. All carried out with my constantly available help, strength and peace. I am a good Master; the best there is. A good prayer, so in line with my heart, is that those I've chosen may see this and draw near. I am in a bonded relationship with my servants. I am not a distant dispenser of tasks and judgments.

Israel, No Longer Ashamed – Day 16

Oh, yes — the great deception. The enemy of souls uses shame to separate my people from me, when it can instead draw us together so beautifully, with such bonding. He teaches them to hide and look away when feeling ashamed, in fearful expectation of judgment and further shame and separation. Yet, those who look to me in the midst of their shame and fear and anger find compassion and undying love, a shame-honor reversal, redemption, and radiant joy. Thank you for participation in calling my people to go against those first inclinations, to look to me, to wait trustingly for my redemption and intervention. This process brings *me* joy, too!

Justice – Day 17

Waiting and longing and watching for me, even in (*especially in*) unjust circumstances, is *always* rewarded — eventually. I am a righteous judge — a faithful, loving, merciful and self-sacrificing one. I will put things to right — someday, somehow. Tune your heart, and its eyes, to mine. You watch, you wait, you'll see.

Land – Day18

I see and hear my people. I understand their needs, am with them in the midst of their situations, and have tremendous resources and power to help — including land. I am not distant, or slow, though it may sometimes seem so. A father of course makes the decisions about his inheritance gifts. As you remind me of my promises and my gifts, you remind yourself. And you also will be changed as you invite me into *your* personal and corporate experience and histories.

The Lord's Right Hand – Day 19

Fear not about the weakness of your own right hand, your own ability to accomplish, to do righteousness, to protect yourselves. I am well able to do all these things. Yet I am not untouched by your feelings of weakness. I gave my own right hand (and my left) into the hands of men — experiencing the ultimate weakness — in order to show the ultimate strength, and to accomplish the ultimate redemption. Look to, call for, ask for, wait upon, lean upon, receive from and trust in *my* right hand. On behalf of Israel. On behalf of yourselves.

Not Forgotten/Not Forsaken – Day 20

Yes, I am a God of steadfast, *chesed*, covenant-keeping, family-bonded, "through thick and thin" love. It doesn't let go, doesn't forsake, doesn't give up, doesn't quit or get fed up or abandon or run out or slip up in moments of weakness. It is a love like no other, and it is what you need. I am the ultimate Parent, and I am revealed and made known as you experience my faithful care, according to my promises – and as others see the evidence unfold. It is the desire of my heart and my love that all may know me, and rest in the security of my embrace.

Peace of Jerusalem – Day 21

How I long for the shalom of Jerusalem! The quiet rest of all being in right relationship with me, and each other. My Kingdom's ways and values at work. The signature of my Presence being felt. It is a worthy prayer for my capitol; my people. That is truly the place for the Presence of the King.

Provision – Day 22

You are skeptical about this, aren't you? You have known lack, and known of much lack experienced by others. That which *is* provided is from me — you can accept that? That which is *not* provided calls for faith — knowing who I am. Not wavering in that personal knowledge and connection. Times of lack deepen this faith, and so they have their place in my economy. Knowing me better can happen when you abound, *and* when you are abased — as you trust, seek and wait upon me. I am a good Father and provider — you, and they, too, can rely on me.

Rebuilding – Day 23

I am all about restoration. Where there is much brokenness there is much opportunity for my best work. I equip my people for the work of repair, rebuilding, replanting, restoring and even rejoicing, as well. Restoring communities, peoples, generations and homes is central to my purposes and my work of redemption. Ruin does not have the last word!

Rejoice with Jerusalem – Day 24

I rejoice in this community of shalom — my people, bonded together in and with me, forever. In covenant; in love which will never let go, and never end. This is the joy set before me for and by which I endured the cross. It is this joy that will be your strength, too. Keep not only this beautiful *vision* in front of you, but the *reality* of joyful bonds in me, my love, and with my people. And, yes — rejoice in my unique relationship with Jerusalem. It will encourage you to know and see my fidelity.

Remember/Recount – Day 25

I know how it benefits you, my children, to keep before you who I am — in the midst of a world of sin and brokenness that easily leads you to forget. My instructions are for your good, and enhance our intimacy. Which is good for both of us. The evidence, witness and testimony of others — especially of my faithfulness to Israel — is something undeniable and therefore concrete for you to hold onto when all else seems to be shifting sand.

Restoration – Day 26

I find restoration to be even more beautiful than my original blessing, creation, provision. It takes extra skill, redemption, cost, time, understanding. It brings forth deeper beauty, and greater awe and appreciation for the restorer. *And* original designer. Greater joy between me and my people, as we rejoice together. This is my work, my plan, my mission. Yes, do please join me in this work of restoration.

Righteousness – Day 27

It is not possible for you to establish your own righteousness. It is an impossibly heavy burden — you would be crushed by the weight of it. Let me carry it, child. I, alone, am strong enough. Follow me, stay with me, receive from me, and you will grow to be more and more like me. Look to my face, which looks on you with joy and faithful love through this atoning work of my Son. Call my people Israel to look, receive and walk free with me, too.

Shalom – Day 28

My plan for Jerusalem, and for all people, is shalom. My shalom. Not a human peace, but a wholeness of everything in the right amount, the good and right way, the right time, and so many more "rights" that it is out of reach without my presence, guidance, and provision. My King, the Messiah, is tasked with bringing this peace of my Kingdom to all who will receive it. Rest in me — and pray for my peace to be extended.

Shepherd — Aliyah – Day 29

Yes, my desire as a Shepherd is to prosper and protect my sheep. The little ones are as much value to me as the big. The lost ones as much as the found. And my heart is deeply stirred by little, lost and scattered ones. Sheep need their own safe place to live and to grow together. This is my purpose and my work. And that of my helpers. I will guide, I will search out, I will draw, I will feed. Thank you for noticing, for asking, and for trusting.

The Spirit – Day 30

My breath, my Spirit, gives life. CPR to the soul. And even the community, and all creation. I *will* breathe life into my people, Israel. Spiritual life. And the repercussions will be glorious. And this is true life — that they may intimately and personally know me, and the One, Yeshua the Messiah, whom I sent.

Waiting – Day 31

Waiting is trusting. Waiting is trustful dependence. It is a posture of the heart. And the attention — trained upon me. Waiting, therefore, serves you — and me — well. I would be happy to teach you to wait. And to draw it out of my people. I will not disappoint!

Acknowledgements

F irst of all, I would like to thank my Dad who really felt for the Jewish people and the nation of Israel. He saw all that was written in Scripture, especially in Ezekiel 37 and Romans 9–11, and he tried to communicate that to anyone who would listen. It took a while, but he finally got through to me. And Mom nurtured all of this with her gentle love for the people and the land.

Hearing Steve Lightle at an Operation Exodus USA conference in 2007 was pivotal in understanding Israel and the importance of Aliyah, as was reading *Operation Exodus* by Gustav Scheller.

I appreciated how Uncle Arne Kvaalen, masterful artist himself, helped me and many others see Israel's place in God's masterful sketch of history.

I am thankful to have my wife Kim along on this journey and have been touched by the listening prayer responses she wrote (see Appendix.)

Israel tours led by Peter Tsukahira, Dr. Larry and Mary Ehrlich, and Yoni Gerrish brought out in new ways the beauty of the land, the people and the Word.

Our North Heights Bless Israel prayer group has provided wonderful fellowship and encouragement over the years; thank you Barbara, Rand and Barb, Joanne, Lynn, Geoff and Holly and others; and North Heights for your support.

Finally, I would like to thank the Lord for the privilege of joining him in something so close to his heart.

About the Author

Christopher Carlson has been leading prayer groups for Israel since 2008 and is an intercessor with Operation Exodus USA. He is a semi-retired family physician living in the Twin Cities with his wife Kimberly, and they have one adult son, David. As God has stirred the author's heart, he has developed a desire for Israel to experience all the fullness of God's promises through Messiah, and for the "watchmen" that God has called to be equipped and encouraged.